A Dozen Delightful Dachshund Tales:

True Stories Including Doxie Angels, War Wieners and Canine Inspirations

By Mike Szymanski

Doxie Tales, Kindle Book 1

To all the Dogs I've know before.
This isn't about just little Dachshunds,
my favorite breed of dog, but about all dogs,
and all pets.

(Doxies, Dora, Rudi, Charly, Rex and Seal, courtesy of Johnny Ortez-Tibbels)

I've lived with and loved Cocker Spaniels, Labrador Retrievers, Australian Shepherds, Standard Poodles, Afghans, Collies, even a Catahoula, and also have loved many non-specific shelter dogs we could never figure out what they were. I've also lived with and loved many, many cats of all shapes, sizes and colors, a Bearded Dragon, Tarantula, Mouse, Hamster, Fish and a Pot-bellied Pig. They were all wonderful, and I cherished my time with them.

These mini books are about love. They are about loving creatures who need our help and depend on us, but these books are a tribute to how they end up giving so much back, and love us unconditionally.

Please share and enjoy . . .

A portion of the sales of these mini-Doxie books go to D.O.G.S. (Dachshund Outreach Giving & Socialization). For more about that non-profit charity see Chapter 3: *He's a Professional Dachshund Photographer: Just Wiener Dogs!*) Look for upcoming books, and I'd love to hear from you at **DachshundExaminer@yahoo.com**.

Table of Contents

***

A Little Dachshund Miracle: How Dogs Know When it's Time to Go

This is a true story about our Dachshund puppy, Charly, and our beloved Australian Shepherd, Miki. Unfortunately, or fortunately, this is exactly what happened.

(I originally wrote this only a few days after it happened.)

Charly is a girl pup, the runt of a three-dog

litter only five weeks ago by our rare all-black Dachshund named Dora. (When you present a boy with a girl puppy and ask him to name her, these days you'll most likely get something like Dora, as in "Dora the Explorer.")

The daddy is named Rex (but actually his name was Zorro when we first got him). Zorro was too close to sounding like Dora, so when we called either name, both ran to us. It got a bit confusing.

"Rex" was part of Zorro's very long official registered breed name, so we took that part of it, and he seemed to like it.

We wanted Rex and Dora — two rare all-black Dachshunds — to have one litter and one litter only. It was planned to be an educational, family experience for my nephews Dante, 14, and Donovan, 8. I think in retrospect, they will agree that it was a memorable moment for them.

When I was their age in Oak Cliff, Texas, a litter of puppies by our little Dachshund-like black dog Jody was a life-changing childhood experience that taught me so many things. Particularly, how to care for others, and take care of life more fragile than ours.

Charly is the only one of our Dachshunds who played with Miki, the bigger, fun-loving dog who was always attached to a tennis ball. Miki could chase a tennis ball for hours, and Charly plodded behind him trying to chew on the ball when she could get to it. Their last night together, both dogs snuggled on a pillow near the boys' beds.

Charly is mischievous and at one point the next day I saw her chewing on a wire that was connected to a computer. I immediately checked the wire, and ran through the house telling everyone to watch for loose phone cords and other wires that the pups may chew on or pull out. We needed to be more careful.

That evening, we found Charly convulsing on a pillow, frothing at the mouth, shaking and whining.

We searched the house for poisons, we searched for plants she may have chewed on, we checked the computer wires. My thought was that she may have been electrocuted, or maybe hit her head on a metal table, or smashed her body against the glass door.

We rushed her to an emergency animal center, where they were rather thorough, but offered us only bad news. Charly suffered from a seizure that impaired her vision. Her pupils and responses were abnormal. She would be given fluids and painkillers and made comfortable, but she would probably not make it through the night. They would keep us informed, but there was nothing else to be done. Estimated cost: $1,600.

It was hard to imagine that Charly would not survive the night. I said "good-bye," watching Charly whining with a high-pitched plaintive cry, connected to IVs and laying in an incubator-like container that I thought would be her tomb. It was heart-breaking.

It was even tougher to tell the news to the boys.

When I came back home, Miki seemed particularly concerned that I hadn't brought back Charly. Miki jumped up on me, tugging at the empty blanket that I carried Charly away in.

Miki whimpered, took the blanket in his mouth and crawled onto the pillow they shared earlier in the evening.

It was close to midnight that night when we got

a call from the emergency center to update us on Charly, and they said X-rays showed no fractures. Her pupils were tiny and even if she survived she may be handicapped, or completely blind. It still didn't look good.

As I sat down to write about it on Facebook, I looked over to our lovely, loyal Australian Shepherd and he stood up from his pillow on wobbly legs and looked over at me with his big brown eyes. I saw Miki fall over and collapse, not far from the spot where Charly was found having the seizure. Miki, an 11-year-old dog in good health, but a bit overweight, couldn't stand up at all. His tongue was gray and he put his head on my lap and whimpered.

I woke up my sister and the oldest boy, Dante, who knew Miki since he was 3. We comforted him, but very quickly, Miki died of an apparent heart attack with all of us around him.

Then, a call came from the emergency center, and they said, "Charly's pupils are getting a bit bigger. She is responding to light. She may make it through the night, but she won't be a normal dog. We may still have to put her down."

Great, I sighed. I told them we just lost our old shepherd only minutes before. They said that that's exactly when they noticed the first signs of new life in Charly.

The next morning, 8-year-old Donovan said good-bye to Miki and then wanted to come to the emergency clinic to say good-bye to Charly. The doctors there recommended that we either take her to a neurologist, or put her down by our regular veterinarian. They didn't want me to take her home to die there peacefully.

Charly was on IVs and medicine and had a catheter in her and I was told if she didn't get reconnected within one hour, she would die. They made arrangements with our vet, where Charly was born after an induced labor because Charly was a runt and just didn't want to come out of Dora, even a day after Dora gave birth to the other two.

"If patient's condition does not improve, recommend euthanasia," is what the dog's report said.

We gave Donovan the option to stay with Charly, or go to school. I urged school, and Donovan asked that if we had to put her to sleep, could he be there, too. I reluctantly agreed.

I came home, and Donovan's dad, John was angry and frustrated that after that night of drama, all that the dog experts could do was recommend putting the pup down.

Adept at handling emergencies with our dogs in

the past, John took out the catheter himself, against doctor's orders. He stopped the bleeding, and eventually, Charly stopped the whining.

We put Charly down on the floor with both her mother and father licking her obsessively, then her brother and sister jumped on her and they all crowded her on their pillow. We expected the end to come soon, but at least Charly would be happy.

As the pet crematory service took Miki's body away, we noticed how Charly seemed to get better.

That afternoon, Donovan came home from school and opened up the door. Mom and dad Doxies ran to greet him, then the two pups, then Charly. Donovan squealed with delight.

We thought Charly still wouldn't make it, but it's been a few days now, and she seems as

normal as ever. We also found out that mini-Dachshunds can be prone to seizures. Unfortunately, little can be done about that.

My sister believes that somehow, the spirit of our old, loyal Miki has transferred into the little runt pup Charly. Miki knew it was his time, and he wanted Charly to live on because she just got here.

The doctors believe it's nothing short of a miracle.

We're just happy that Charly seems safe, and happy.

(Epilogue: Charly is now 9 years old, and has never had a seizure since. She is athletic, a fast ball chaser, and a favorite at the dog park where she frequently has a ball in her mouth that's bigger than her head. When she sees an Australian Shepherd, she drops the ball and snuggles up with it immediately. She has never forgotten Miki, and has inherited the ball-chasing skills of her late mentor.)

***

Doxie Angels: Dachshunds That Love to Visit Nursing Homes

I know that when my Mom lived in a nursing home, she always loved it when I brought in Rudi, our red Doxie who was 16 years old at the time (or 112 in human years).

"This dog is older than any of us here," Mom would announce to her friends. Mom was in a wheelchair, suffering paralysis on the right side of her body after a severe stroke. "If this dog can make it, we can all make it."

Old graying Rudi loved to visit and pranced around the whole place, fascinated by all the smells, and wagged his tail as people reached from their beds or wheelchairs to pet, or pick him up to snuggle. It seemed perk him up after he recently lost his longtime companion, Pepe.

My mom was afraid of cats, especially black cats. There was a rumor around many nursing homes that if they saw a black cat walk outside their window or somewhere on the grounds, that person would die within 24 hours. She swore it was true. The story was even in the news.

"But Rudi is safe, he is a good pet to see," Mom insisted to her friends. "Look, he is active, he is alive, and he's 112. Older than anyone on this floor. Older than anyone in this facility."

Dachshunds are perfect for taking to nursing homes. They are small, they're usually not threatening, and often cause people to squeal about how cute they are.

That proved to be true in other places as well, so I learned. I got to interview a Doxie mama, D.R. Raff who lives in Palm Desert, California and owns two rescue Dachshunds named Chava Rose and Shaina.

They have a heart-wrenching story of how they become an inseparable team. They love to play together, and they love to dress up. They also love to visit the elderly.

And so, Raff takes the pups to the local nursing homes, where lonely, elderly people generally have nothing else to do except watch TV and stay out of the Southern California desert heat. It's a wclcome distraction when Raff and the comical pair of Dachshunds come in to get a whole bunch of love from strangers. The dogs bask in the attention, much like Rudi.

"My girls love visiting the local nursing homes," Raff said. "They are a great hit. They also visit private homes where there are shut-ins. They bring such happiness."

Raff has lived with Dachshunds all her 73 years. "I rescued and placed Dachshunds for

many years," Raff said.

Of course, in the case of these two, it's a special and wonderful story. It's a case of each of them finding each other.

"Chava Rose adopted me eight years ago," Raff said. "A mistreated show-dog, she was 3 years old, and had still-born pups. Then, she was thrown out for not having salable live puppies."

The story was heartbreaking. Chava Rose was deeply traumatized. It was very obvious to Raff.

"She was quiet and had no idea what to do when having choices," Raff said.

Perhaps it was out of fear, or just insecurity. The dog just sat where she was set down on the ground and then was afraid to move.

“She was as sweet as could be, but very over-trained,” Raff mused.

When Chava Rose went to the veterinarian, she was checked out and X-rayed. They found one collapsed kidney and many other health issues. The vet did a C-section and removed still-borns, and she had a raging infection.

“She slowly recovered and began to show a precious personality,” Raff said. “She was still quiet, yet loving. She learned to climb the four steps up to my bed.”

About one year later, Chava was at a neighbor’s house playing with the three Doxies living there. Raff was called over to the neighbor’s house and told to come over immediately to see what her dog was doing.

Raff was surprised because she never knew

Chava to have done anything wrong. Instead, she was delighted.

“I went over immediately only to find her with an eight-week old pup trying to nurse it," Raff said.

Chava Rose was acting on her instincts that she was never able to fulfill with her own pups.

"So I took her on a search to find her baby,” Raff said. “After we searched she found little Shaina who was only months old with a cast on one front leg. They fell in love.”

Chava Rose is obviously dealing with the loss of her past still-born litters. Now, she’s making up for it.

Raff said, “Chava Rose is the best Mom ever. She washes her pup twice a day and sleeps wrapped around her pup.”

These Dachshunds are tiny, even for miniatures. Chava Rose is nine pounds, one ounce and 11 years old now. Shaina Sprientz is seven pounds and two ounces. They are both very long and very short, even for the breed.

They like dressing up. They especially like their bumble-bee costumes.

But around the holidays, the Dachshunds are particular hits in their angel costumes in the nursing home. They make their rounds with their wings and halos.

People love them, and it may bring their only smile of the day. Sometimes, a few of them tell them that the Dachshunds are the only visitors some of the people have had in years. Many regulars enjoy seeing the dogs on a frequent basis.

Raff says, “I know what they mean to me. I feel it is the least I can do.”

“They are my angels, and they make people smile.”

***

The Truth and Legends of the Wiener Village in Bavaria

Even today, the legends persist about the "Dachshund Village of the World" in Bavaria, where the tiny village of Gergweis makes the claim for being the official breeding center for Dachshunds since 1929.

At one point, the city claimed to have two Dachshunds for every human when it was a town of 1,000 people. And, while that is no longer true (if it

ever was in the first place), a lot of tall tales still exist for the long dog in the little town.

It has incorrectly been credited as the place where most of the Dachshunds were originally bred, or where the breed was perfected. A 1957 black-and-white Pathe News reel done right after WWII helped perpetuate the myth of the "Dachshund Village."

The truth is that in the 1920s, a breeder named Kathi Dorfmeister brought the dogs to town and became such a success, it bred a number of competitors. But, a terrible viral epidemic decimated the dog population in 1938 and killed 400 of the dogs in the village, leaving only 10 in the kennels.

But, they continued on, and during WWII the Dachshunds served as watchdogs at farms surrounding the town, which led to a favorite Dackel legend in Gergweis.

At 3 in the morning of May 1, 1945, the American forces were sweeping over Germany, but apparently were scared off in Gergweis by an onslaught of furiously barking Dachshunds. The old-timers insist the dogs scared away the soldiers.

Back in 1968, a farmer named Ludwig Knodl sold the long-sized dogs and ran a hotel when tiny Doxie-sized beds in every room.

Dogs also had their own special menu for meals, and of course the specialty was Wiener Schnitzel.

Also, tourists without a dog could rent one by the hour. They could also rent a rowboat.

Knodl himself did not own a Dachshund, although plenty of neighbors around allowed their Dachshunds to be used, and the German National Tourist Board created a DZT time which stood for "Dachshunds Per Hour." Some animal lovers complained about the renting practice, and said it was dog exploitation.

One article in a national German paper proclaimed: "Dog Lovers All Over Germany Horrified About Gergweis Dachshund Rental."

But the International Dackelclub made sure the practice in Gergweis consisted of merely walking a dog around with a leash, and not over-taxing the hounds.

The city has a legendary "Lord Gergweis" that is a Dachshund who lives along the wooded riverfront and goes on adventures. Poems, songs and stories recount the tales of Lord Gergweis.

Although the national Dachshund museum is not here (but it is close by in another town in Bavaria), you can still have a wiener-ful time in Gergweis.

***

He's a Professional Dachshund Photographer: Just Wiener Dogs!

Some people make a living photographing food. Some photographers specialize in medical photography, or chasing celebrities, or shooting weddings or kids.

Johnny Ortez-Tibbels has carved out a very specialized niche with his photography—he takes pictures of Dachshunds, only Doxies.

© Tibbels & Tibbels 2013

And Johnny is somewhat of a Dachshund Whisperer of sorts, able to get some of the wildest little long dogs to simmer down and pose for a photo. He is able to capture their looks, smiles, even character after spending long hours with each dog, and using his own Doxie muse, Rufus, to help make the subject feel comfortable.

"I'm a big fan of the Dachshund, they have a unique body type and are a small dog with a big personality," said Johnny who lives in Southern California, and typically has a Doxie play date with other dogs running around.

"They're a magical breed," he insisted. And, he adds quickly, something that people don't like to always talk about, "The dog poop is small, and so it's manageable." That's a consideration when picking a dog.

That's why you see Dachshunds in cities like New York and Chicago where apartment dwellers live in high rises. "You can wash them in the sing, they are easy to travel with, and yo can take them on planes," Johnny said.

His old red Doxie Rufus has traveled to New York, Chicago, New Mexico and Texas. During one trip, they hit 15 states in 20 days.

"Dachshunds are a bold and noble breed," explained Johhny, "but they are not for everyone. They can be high maintenance."

The breed can suffer problems with their teeth, eyes, and most importantly, their back. They surely for a Dachshund's back goes for about $8,000 and it has to be done within the first 72 hours of the injury, or some experts say thc dog could be in a wheelchair device for the rest of its life because it's hind legs are useless.

Johnny started D.O.G.S, the Dachshund Outreach Giving and Socialization nonprofit charity that concentrates in the eduction of the complex breed, and helps some people with their cost of surgeries and back treatments. "We use original photos as a means to entertain and educate, to initiate discourse in our community and to get one another talking about each other's experiences — the good, the bad, and the in between," Johnny

© Johnny Ortez-Tibbels | www.rufusontheweb.com

explained.

"We are help those Dachshunds in need after proper vetting through our program, and advocate regular and routine socialization for the long-bodied, short-legged winer dogs."

The breed requires some specialized knowledge and information, and they collaborate with multiple rescues and vendors and other Doxie groups like Dodger's List and Dachshund Delights. With the help of some charitable arts organizations, Johnny created a beautiful one-of-a-kind 104-page all-color picture book called ***102 Dachshunds***, and the proceeds went to the D.O.G.S. charity.

Johnny insists that he wasn't a Dachshund person—or even an animal person—but then 11 years ago he met his partner, film producer Kirkland Tibbels of Funny Boy Films. Kirkland had Dachshunds while growing up, and wanted to get a dog.

They tried a Beta fish first, and then Johnny warmed up to getting a dog. It was his first dog, a sweet red named Rufus, and they also got a black-and-tan rescue Dachshund named Emily, and another red, Lily.

"Dachshunds are always among the top 10 favorite breeds in the U.S.," Johnny noted. "They are such a diverse breed, there are three different official coat types, there are different sizes, and they live an average of 15 to 20 years, which is a lot longer than most breeds."

For Johnny, having a Dachshund was what he said a mother must feel for a child—unconditional love. Rufus has been declared an "emotional support" dog, so he can be brought in to places that don't normally allow dogs.

Johnny photographs with a selfie stick, and a device that allows him to get down with the Doxie-eye level, and shoots with a Canon single reflex camera. He received a print journalism degree from

the University of Texas at Arlington and has literally taken thousands of photos of every kind and color of Dachshund you can imagine.

"I've been photographing Dachshunds since Rufus was a pup and over the years I have really come to appreciate the breed's natural beauty and grace," Johnny said. "I think my love for these comical and loyal low-riders is reflected in my pictures."

People from all over the world visit RufusOnTheWeb.com just to get their Daily Dose of Doxie, and smile even in the roughest of times.

Writes one reader, Laurie, on his site: “I enjoy your photos every day, they always make me smile. I have 3 beautiful doxies myself…they are a unique breed!”

Johnny hosts monthly meet-ups with a group called L.A. Doxies, and they get scored of

Dachshunds of all shapes and sizes to gather at different locations every month in Southern California, and on the dog beach at least once a year.

The dog photographer said, "I'm just enjoying the art of photographing my breed of choice and sharing them with my fellow doxie-holics."

Research is important for anyone who wants to adopt a dog, and D.O.G.S. is around to help anyone figure out if the Dachshund is a good fit for them.

"It is a loyal breed, but Dachshunds are hard to train," said Johnny, who has taken Rufus to two obedience courses. "They are independent thinkers and stubborn. They are the smallest of hunters. If you don't invest the time and energy with them, then you will be disappointed."

For the first 30 days, Johnny explains, he spent nearly full-time with Emily to train her and housebreak her.

“I spend time with them, to get to know them,” said Johnny. And that’s what he does during the play dates he has when people leave their Doxies to play with Emily, Lily and Rufus.

Now, in 2020, sadly, Johnny spends almost full-time with Rufus, who is dying of a kidney disease and for more than a year, Johnny has been posting a "Long Good-Bye" for 16-year-old Rufus. Living much longer than the veterinarians imagined, Rufus has been subject to daily injections and treatments, and Johnny takes Rufus out multiple times a night. Johnny takes Rufus everywhere, and Rufus doesn't seem to mind.

"We’re just happy to have him with us, for as long as he wants to stay with us," Johnny said.

Meanwhile, is there enough work for a Dachshund photographer?

"There are some pretty fanatical people about Dachshunds out there," he smiles. "They collect everything Dachshund. I hope some of them like my photos, too."

***

Remembering War Wieners: Brave Dachshunds that Served in the Military

Believe it or not, our four-legged friends joined soldiers on the battlefield, often for comfort, but also for strategic combat assistance.

Sure, you hear about Collies, or German Shepherds, Saint Bernards or Pit Bulls doing heroic feats in times of war, but there are a number of Dachshunds who were trained for the battlefront, too.

At the end of WWII, two notable Dachshunds named Berta and Herman von Hildensheim served as mine detection dogs. The brave pair of dogs are credited with having uncovered more than 600 land mines throughout Europe, mostly in Italy, toward the end of the war.

They were registered in the Dogs for Defense program which was run out of the Office fo Strategic Services, and a predecessor to the Central Intelligence Agency. Doxies were also known to serve in the K-9 Corps as well during WWII.

Known incidents of Dachshunds in combat date back to World War I, and unfortunately records show that the dogs were often on the wrong side of history, and therefore often maligned.

In WWI, Kaiser Wilhelm II was known for his love of the breed, but that led to a drop in its

popularity in the United States.

In WWII, Dachshunds were used Germans for tasks like seeking bombs, and finding food under armored vehicles. Sometimes, the dogs were starved and the sent to battlefields with explosives attached to them, which is so horrible in itself, but so was how the breed was ostracized by Americans.

Because they are associated with Germany, both World Wars put serious strains on the breed in the States, and having a Doxie became taboo.

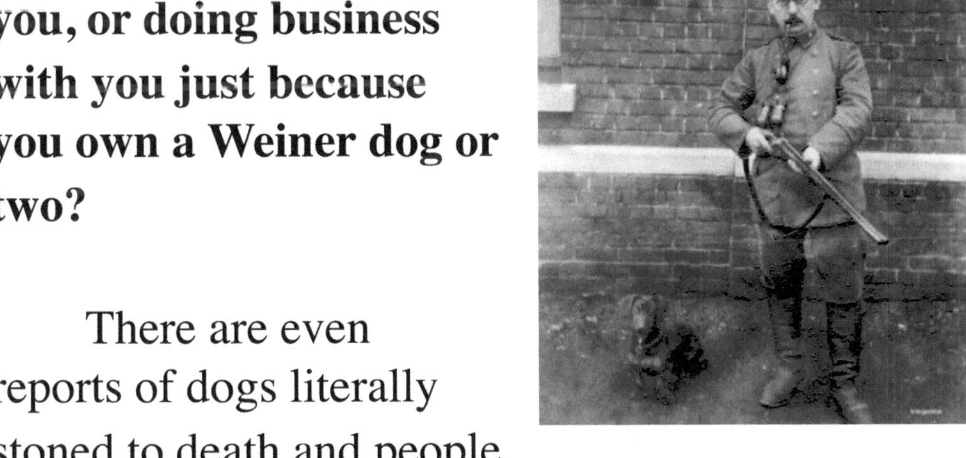

Can you imagine someone not speaking to you, or doing business with you just because you own a Weiner dog or two?

There are even reports of dogs literally stoned to death and people banished from communities for owning and breeding Dachshunds.

It got so bad that anything German was equated with disloyalty. Sauerkraut became "Liberty

cabbage," German measles became "Liberty measles," and **Dachshunds were re-branded as "Liberty pups."**

And so, the national American Kennel Club tried to change the name of Dachshund to "Badger

Dogs" (it literally means "badger hound" in German), and they also tried "Wiener dogs," but they didn't quite catch on.

The breed became so shunned that the classic movie "Wizard of Oz" was originally written to have a Dachshund named Otto in it when it was being filmed in 1938. But, with the pressures of the German taboo, they recast the part to a Cairn Terrier and rearranged the scripted name of Otto and named it Toto.

A disturbing notation of Dachshunds in the German military came with a diary entry by the son of Field Marshall Rommel in 1944, who was forced to commit suicide. The boy detailed the final moments of Rommel's life, which included saying good-bye to his dog:

"My father put his wallet carefully back in his pocket. As he went into the hall, his little

Dachshund which he had been given as a puppy a few months before in France, jumped up at him with a whine of joy.

'Shut the dog in the study, Manfred,' he said, and waited in the hall with Aldinger while I removed the excited dog and pushed it through the study door.

Then we walked out of the house together.

In a vintage photo of WWII, two American American soldiers are shown, one with a Dachshund on his lap and one with a pet raccoon resting on his shoulder.

Dachshunds were easy to take into combat because they could move fast, didn't require as much food, could easily burrow under barbed wire and remained loyal to their masters.

According to the military Hulton Archives, the long-dog breed was "good for the morale of the troops, and many soldiers took this breed to the front as a short-term pet. The UK and the U.S. Army Corps had them as their mascot as well.”

Pfc. Floyd Gantzer in the 17th Airborne fought in the Battle of the Bulge in Belgium in January 1945. He wrote about how dogs were used in combat support for years and detailed 24 breeds, including Doxies, that were used in both the German and American armies.

Gantzer writes about the Dachshund he acquired:

“I found a mother Dachshund that was about to die and she had five just-born babies. I got some powdered milk and fed them with an eye dropper,” he said.

“Two of them lived. I gave one to the mess sergeant in Berlin and I kept the other one."

“I called him Mike. I brought him home with me on the Queen Mary. No animals were allowed to come back to the States on the ship, so I hid him in my duffel bag."

"You should have seen all the dogs running around on the deck of the ship the second day at sea,” the old soldier said with a grin.

***

Making a Movie with Six Dachshunds Is Like, Well, Herding Cats

Writer, journalist, activist and filmmaker Nicole Kristal loves her little red Dachshund named Lola, and that was the first surefire part she gave when casting her first movie. Lola got a guaranteed a part.

Nicole wrote a movie about a young bisexual woman who is dating both men and women, but also that woman is severely allergic to cats. She goes through a series of relationships with guys and gals she really likes, but if they have a cat, that's a deal-breaker.

The character, like Nicole for real, breaks out in hives and itches if there's a cat anywhere nearby. It's a story based on some of the comical dating experiences of Nicole, who is also noted bisexual activist and educator.

The female character falls for a woman who also falls for Nicole's dog. Lola has never been smart enough to avoid running in front of moving cars, and that ended up being a huge asset for this shoot. Lola almost being hit by a car is how the two women meet in the movie.

Personally, I loaned the production five dogs to join Lola for the final, very hysterical, sequence. But working with all the dogs is a challenge.

Comedian and film star W.C. Fields once warned, “Never work with children or animals,” and many famed directors found themselves severely challenged when dealing with pets on the set.

Director of this short film, Jason Sax, recalled the ordeal:

“I’m surprised the neighbors didn’t call the cops, because we were screaming bloody murder to get the dogs to follow us inside."

The director added, "We tried a couple of times and finally got one take done to our liking. Without replaying the tape, I knew we’d gotten the shot, and fortunately wouldn’t have to try again.”

The short film, ***"Do You Have a Cat?"*** won many awards, and screened around the world. It showed at the Palm Springs International ShortFest, Frameline36: The San Francisco International LGBT Film Festival and FilmOut San Diego, where it won the Best Female Short. It received international praise and played at the Oslo Gay & Lesbian Film Festival, Philadelphia QFest, Indiana Cares Campaign Film Festival, image+nation Montréal International LGBT Film Festival, Barcelona LGBT Short Film Festival and many others. (You can see more about the film at www.DoYouHaveACat.net.)

Nicole (and me) are co-authors of the Lambda-award-winning book "The Bisexual's Guide the the Universe: Quips, Tips & Lists for those who Go Both Ways" which is one of the first places she wrote about her dating experiences, and then she wrote the short film about being an allergy-prone bisexual.

Nicole landed actress Amber Benson as part of the cast, and she is best known for her role as the bisexual character “Tara” on Buffy the Vampire Slayer. She eagerly joined the cast and wanted to be part of the film.

“We were willing to offer her any part. She wanted to play the best friend, and we were thrilled because of her natural comedic timing,” said Nicole.

The casting process for the lead was much more challenging. Nicole was concerned with finding a believable bisexual girl. They auditioned several people with the right look, but none of them had the chops. Then, they found Samantha Sloyan, who at the time didn't have many credits, but ended up becoming very well known.

“Everytime we watch the film, we realize it was the best decision we made,” said Sax

Red-headed Sloyan, went on to get a regular role in "Grey's Anatomy" and starred in "The Haunting of Hill House."

Director Sax has gone on to worked as visual effect producer on "The Walking Dead," "Episodes" and "Grimm" as well as working on TV shows such as "Fringe" and "Eleventh Hour."

The film was pretty low-budget, but the biggest expenditure was the $1,100 needed for Hollywood cats to perform in two scenes. Nicole asked for a special grant from the charitable foundation the California Institute of Contemporary Arts to help get a cat to do what she needed it to do. You simply can't take a cat out of its environment and tell it what to do. (They tried with a number of untrained cats.)

"The Hollywood cats showed up and the trainers were very upset the van had to be parked

about a hundred feet from the wooded bungalow in Echo Park where we shot, so we had to make our producer babysit the cats so they'd be comfortable," said Nicole.

"Trey, who like me and Jason, is deathly allergic to cats, alternated between sneezing his ass off in the van and sitting outside shivering for several hours. But the cats made their cues perfectly and were worth every penny," Nicole said.

"Of course, the dogs, well, they are Dachshunds after all, but hey, they were free, and they did a fine job," Nicole laughed. "Some would say they're the best part of the movie."

***

7 Fun Facts About the First Olympic Mascot—Waldi, the Dachshund

The first mascot of any Olympic Games wasn't until 1972 in Munich, and the symbol depicted turned out to be Germany's might Dachshund.

Since then, pandas, eagles, beavers, tigers, sperm-like characters and ridiculous computer-graphic fantasy characters also served as mascots, but Waldi was the first.

Here are seven fun facts about the first Olympic mascot, Waldi, the Dachshund:

1. Waldi was modeled after a real long-haired Dachshund named Cherie von Birkenhof, who was a dog that the Munich Games

Organizing Committee president gave to the International Sports Press Association President two years before the Olympics.

2. Waldi was created by designer Otl Aicher who

also is credited with designing the logo for German airline Lufthansa.

3. The Olympic committee picked a **Dachshund because the breed has qualities that make a great athlete: resistance, tenacity and agility**.

4. Waldi's colors were blue and stripes of the Olympics, except those of the National Socialist Party (so no red or black was allowed).

5. The way the route of the marathon in those Olympics was designed used the Waldi design. The

course was modeled like the map of a dog, with the head of the dog facing toward the West, and the athletes ran counter-clockwise, starting at the back of the dog's neck and continuing around the ears through Nymphenburg Park. The stomach was the main downtown in Munich and the rear and tail were in the English Gardens.

6. More than 2 million Waldi-related items were made and sold, including a plush toy, a plastic toy, buttons, posters, stickers, and a pin. It helped fund the games, and some of the buildings plan for them.

7. The popularity of Waldi caused future Olympic committees to come up with their own mascots and brands to help raise money.

***

Ammo the Adventurous, Artistic Dachshund Takes Flight

Can your Doxie fly? Meet a most amazing Dachshund named Ammo. He paddleboats, flies and is an artist, and you can buy his art! (A portion of it goes to charity.)

This dog is a charmer from Downingtown, Pennsylvania and on his blog, his "mom" Kyley DiLuigi, are shown doing all kinds of crazy stunts and going on exciting adventures.

The best is seeing Ammo scratch out his living by scratching some colors on a canvas and enjoying creating his own art.

Ammo's primary job since 2008 is being the

official store greeter at the customer frame shop Studio 3 in the heart of Downingtown. He's also the sidekick to the Painting Ponies, the team of Kyley's talented Chincoteague ponies that create paintings for charity.

Not to be outdone, or just wanting to join in the fun, Ammo used his paws to create his own water color masterpieces that have been framed and displayed around the world.

As Ammo puts it:

"I not only take on the role of one and only dog at my home in Pennsylvania, but I also help run my mom's business as official store greeter at her small custom frame shop in town. When I'm not busy saying hello to my adoring fans at the shop I am the sidekick to the talented Painting Ponies at the family farm.

I love to 'horse around' with the ponies – sometimes performing tricks with them in their acts. My antics with the ponies even landed me on Animal Planet's America's Cutest Dogs."

Ammo started his scratch art in May 2010 and in a few months became known as the World's First Painting Dachshund.

Some of the money for Ammo's art goes to charity; the Main Line Animal Rescue, the SPCA and other charities.

Ammo is a 17-pound red dapple whose favorite food is hot dogs and cheese, and favorite trick is playing dead. He became a certified canine good citizen and therapy dog in 2012.

Kyley takes most of the photos of Ammo, and teaches him new tricks with clicker training. She offers tips of dog agility and basic dog obedience skills.

On his blog you can see Ammo getting into his own single engine plane – a Piper Archer II. **The fearless dog is sticking his snout out the window as they fly over the Marsh Creek Lake where he previously went paddle boarding.** You can see photos and video of that, too.

If you love Dachshunds, or simply love

adventure, check out his award-winning Ammo Blog at ammothedachshund.com.

The blog is not only entertaining for the whole family, but rather informative, including making your do-it-yourself dog toys, identifying skin cancer on your Doxie, and dealing with the introduction of a baby to the family (Ammo's little "sister").

Muses Ammo: "Not gonna lie, it was a big adjustment at first but I'm really starting to enjoy the sweet hugs my sister gives me and our nighttime tug-of-war ritual."

"I have a feeling that my days of princess dress-up and Disney movies are just around the corner. And I'm totally ready!"

***

His Doxie Inspires 'Twilight Saga: Eclipse' Movie Director David Slade

Movie director David Slade is noted for his psycho-sexual thriller "Hard Candy," his graphic novel vampire film "30 Days of Night" and the third "Twilight Saga: Eclipse," starring Kristen Stewart, Robert Pattinson and Taylor Lautner, reprising their roles as Bella Swan, Edward Cullen and Jacob Black.

Slade has also directed and produced

"American Gods" and "Hannibal." Fans may be surprised to know that this British director of harsh material has a softer side, and it's inspired by his Dachshund named Django.

"I am inspired by my German Dachshund Django, who is definitely a design inspiration," said Slade.

In between his psycho thrillers, he draws dog cartoons and created a series of quirky stories about Meatdog, a Dachshund who is made of cuts of meat. His first cartoon short is called:
"Meatdog: What's Fer Dinner"

The story is what Slade calls "fubear," and that's an off-beat sense of humor that's the schism that exists between "funny ha-ha" and "funny-strange." "Fubear" is now a 48-page illustrated by Slade about Meatdog, and an odd cast of characters including Bearleftbear, an obsessive-compulsive

bear in a car, and the Alienbears, who are hungry carnivorous older bears from another universe.

The short movie premiered at ComiCon to widespread praise and then played to seven million users on xBox Live.

“Meatdog” involves a church of evil occult pigs, a carnivorous rabbit, and a slobbering hound in pursuit of the title character. The Fubear Studios hardcover vividly introduces us to not only Meatdog himself, Bearleftbear, the Alienbears, “Drumming Dogs,” and “Hazmat Bears” from a chemical psychoverse.

Some of his art is rather poignant, especially in the series of "Scarfdog Loves Duck" where Scarfdog's love is rejected in an interspecies romance. There's also an art piece of a flying fat Dachshund called "Wiener Blimp," and one of his most popular prints is called "Hanging by the Thread of a Hot Dog."

"Django is my constant audience, always there when I work, and an arbiter of taste," says David. "I couldn't have a better critic."

***

Behind the Scenes of the 'Wiener Dog Nationals' Movie

Filmmaker Kevan Peterson went with his friend Greg Gutierrez to a little-known Southern California event, the Wienerschnitzel Weiner Nationals, a Dachshund-racing event that started off in 2005 as a fundraiser for the no-kill Seal Beach Animal Care Center.

"I was so intrigued with the race, and the fans, and the funny dogs that I thought I had to make a movie about this whole phenomena," says Kevan.

He not only made one, he made two movies about it, called "Wiener Dog Nationals" and "Wiener Dog Internationals," and he used a lot of local Dachshund meet-up groups in the creation of the movies.

The races are sponsored by the fast-foot Der Wienerschnitzel restaurants that specialize in hot dogs.

"We loved the idea of creating a story around the races," Peterson said. "It became a great family film."

The G-rated movie is about a single father, played by Jason London ("Dazed and Confused"). He is bringing up three children who want a dog, and they end up getting a Dachshund.

This particular dog has a marking, making it a prize hound, and an evil dog racer Missy Merryweather, played by Morgan Fairchild ("Dallas" and "Falcon Crest"), wants that dog.

The director also cast a notable Dachshund star, too, Penny Lane, who won many of the Wiener Dog races in the past, and races in the film.

The movie has Missy trying to get their Dachshund by any means necessary and in the meantime, the young son enters Shelly in the Wiener races against their Dad's will.

One of the racing judges is played by actress Melanie Alicia Witt, and she is banned by the head judge played by Brian Batt as she tries to prove with the family that they are cheating. Shelly the Dachshund ends up being a superstar in the races.

The director wanted to make sure that shelter dogs are mentioned in the movie, and pointed out that even well-loved breeds like Dachshunds get abandoned at shelters.

In the movie, the son played by actor Julian Feder finds the dog in a shelter and they pick the runt of a litter and call it "Shelly" because they found her in a shelter.

Director Peterson said he wanted to create a family film "that was a fun ride, and a feel-good film." He kiddingly refers to it as: **"The Seabiscut movie for dogs."**

Peterson said, "We are blown away by the positive response to the film. "

Although he never got a Doxie for a pet, Peterson said he appreciated them after making two films with dozens of them.

"They have a great personality and a great sense of humor," the director said.

"They are the only breed of dog that I can say is ironic," he added.

"And, well, simply, these are the greatest movies ever made, the greatest Wiener Dog movies ever made," Kevan quipped.

***

Obie the Obese Doxie Sheds 52 Pounds in a Year and Becomes a Calendar Model

Fat dogs are a national problem, and Dachshunds are known for eating as much as they can possibly eat. Other breeds will stop eating at some point if you put down too much food.

Dachshunds will eat everything you put down and then beg you for more as if they are starving.

That's how some Dachshunds get overweight, and it's not good for them. It's dangerous for their backs, and their overall health. But, it's a problem with the breed.

According to the Association for Pet Obesity Prevention, an estimated 54 percent of dogs and cats in the United States are overweight or obese.

Those extra pounds can lead to a whole host of preventable medical conditions that could shorten the life of our favorite furriest family members.

Obie, the very large obese Dachshund, made national news for being so big, that news crews followed his story of fantastic weight loss.

The severely overweight Dachshund hit a high mark of 77 pounds because of owners who fed him fast-food hamburgers and couldn't take care of him anymore. The elderly couple that Obie lived with realized that the stubby-legged dog could hardly walk, and dragged his stomach along the ground.

The couple felt sorry because they said that Obie would whine if she wasn't fed constantly. They fed her people food, which is a no-no for any dog.

Some of the neighbors in Portland took the dog in when the couple decided they could no longer handle Obie.

Her new owner, Nora Vanatta, took over the challenged by adopting the dog. Nora took the weight loss challenge to prove that Obie wasn't the biggest loser of the dog world, or maybe could be the biggest loser.

Nora, with the help of many experts, fed and exercised Obie to bring her to an optimal weight of a five-year-old dog.

The dog lost 52 pounds in one year, and is almost exactly the ideal weight of a standard breed of a Dachshund at 25 pounds. There was surgery required to remove excess skin and a prescription diet food.

Obie went on a tour throughout the United States to help promote obesity prevention not only with dogs, but with humans, too. Obie has managed to keep the weight off, too.

"Obie is doing great and holding steady between 22 and 23 pounds for more than a year now," Nora recently posted. "He has some residual fat pockets on his sides and lacks normal muscle tone but is healthy overall."

Once known as Obie, the world’s fattest Dachshund, the dog is now a star in his own calendar model. Obie's new look is featured in a series of calendars that are being used to raise money for Obie's continued health.

What Nora did to help with the weight loss was to stop all of Obie's high-calorie foods that made him pack the pounds, and replaced it with a low-fat, high-protein diet specifically designed to help dogs slim down.

In the first week, Obie dropped seven pounds, but his body wasn't ready to handle the physical work it would require to really take the weight off.

Nora documented the dog’s diet and weight loss journey and Obie became an Internet inspiration. Donations came in to help with Obie’s care Facebook friends reached more than 82,000 fans.

He is a “magical dog” as Nora describes, and she chronicles his progress with photos and weight posts.

"For people struggling with weight loss, or have pudgy dogs, Obie remains a great source of inspiration," Nora said. "We are happy to celebrate Obie's progress."

***

Are Dachshunds a Dying Breed? Study Shows Wieners May Go the Way of the Dodo After a 40-Year Decline

A notable four-decade decline in the number of Dachshund puppies is making some wiener lovers concerned that the sausage dog is destined for extinction and is part of a dying breed.

The German Dachshund Club has shown a decrease in the amount of new puppies bred in Germany for nearly four decades.

A surge of Dachshund breeding followed the 1972 Olympics in Munich because that year's mascot was Waldi, the Dachsie (see Chapter 7). That sparked a high point of 25,000-plus puppies in the country, and that took nearly a decade to subside.

A reporter for a German-based English-language publication *The Local*, interviewed experts at a national Dachshund show and found that the usual demand in breeding the dog has hit an all-time low.

That was a disturbing trend for many of the people interviewed. It was significant because Germany is where the Dachshund originated and bred as a good hunting dog that can burrow underground and catch badgers.

Although people don't tend to get Dachshunds to burrow and hunt badgers anymore, it is distressing that the interest in the ergonomically-challenged dog seems to be waning.

In fact, the German Kennel Club (or VDH) shows a drop of 34 percent in breeding numbers between 1999 and 2008, with new puppies falling from 10,035 to 6,615. In Germany, Dachshunds are still the second-most popular breed, following of course, the German shepherd.

In the United States, the 2009 statistics by the American Kennel Club show that Dachshunds ranks eighth in popularity, falling from the fourth-favorite level in 1999.

The 10-year decline of Dachshund interest is due to a surge in popularity of Boxers, Bulldog sand Yorkshire Terriers during the last decade, according to the statistics.

The lower statistics in breeding are not

necessarily a bad thing, according to dog experts.

One report quotes experts as saying that the decline in the United States simply means that a lot more disreputable dog breeders are being drummed out of business or shut down. That is a good thing.

Some are saying that many Dachshund owners are simply not breeding their dogs and are too lazy to send in their $10 registration dues.

According to the popular Long & Short of It blog about Dachshunds, there is no need for alarm that the lovable Dachshie is going the way of the Dodo bird.

The breed has fallen to number seven as far as the most favorite breed in the country, but that's only from a number six spot that the breed has held for more than a decade.

And of course, ask any Dachshund Rescue group (DRNA.org). There are still plenty of Dachsies to go around.

***

Look for these other ***Doxie Tales*** *books coming up by Mike Szymanski:*

Long & Short Lists of Dachshund Fun Fats: Best Cities, Names, Movies & More About Your Wiener Dog Doxie Tales, Kindle 2

The Levitating Dachshund of Walla Walla and Other Doxie Ghost Stories
Doxie Tales, Kindle 3

Brave Little Dachshund Tales: True Stories of Blind, Wheelchair-bound Canines & More Who Became Heroes Doxie Tales, Kindle 4

Scary Dachshund Tales: Ghost Dogs, Bear attacks, and Justice for a Dog Killer
Doxie Tales, Kindle 5

A Personal Doxie History, Two Old Reds, Two Pure Blacks, Two Unique Blues & A Lot of Love
Doxie Tales, Kindle 6

***

www.ingramcontent.com/pod-product-compliance
Ingram Content Group UK Ltd.
Pitfield, Milton Keynes, MK11 3LW, UK
UKHW041850190726
13854UKWH00002B/818